THE CREATIVE MIND

AN EXPLORATION OF THE SECRETS TO UNLEASH YOUR CREATIVITY

DR. JAGADEESH PILLAI

|| Dedicated to all wisdom seekers around the World ||

Contents

Contents

Prayer

**"Om Bhadram Karnebhih Shrunuyaama
DevaahBhadram Pashyemaakshabhiryajatraah
SthirairangaistushtuvaamsastanoobhihVyashema
Devahitam YadaayuhSwasti Na Indro
VridhashravaahSwasti Nah Pooshaa
VishwavedaahSwasti Nastaarkshyo ArishtanemihSwasti
No Brihaspatir DadhaatuOm Shantih, Shantih, Shantih"**

The literal meaning of this mantra is: OM. O Gods! Let us
hear auspicious words from our ears. O reverent Gods! Let
us behold propitious visions from our eyes, let our organs
and body be stable, healthy, and strong. Let us do that
which is pleasing to the gods in the life span allotted to us.
May Indra, inscribed in the scriptures, bring us fortune!
May Pushan, the knower of the world, grant us prosperity!
May Trakshya, who vanquishes enemies, bestow us with
blessings! May Brihaspati bring us success!
OM Peace, Peace, Peace.

About The Author

Dr. Jagadeesh Pillai is a renowned Guinness World Record holder, writer, and researcher hailing from Varanasi, also known as the abode of Lord Shiva. With a Ph.D. in Vedic Science and a range of creative ideas and achievements, he is a true polymath. He is the author of more than 100 books including Research Publications. Although his roots can be traced back to Kerala, the people of Varanasi hold him in high regard and affectionately consider him one of their own.

In 1998, Dr. Pillai was offered a job at Banaras Hindu University, but he left the position after only two months to pursue greater goals in life. He believed that in order to study Indian scriptures and engage in other creative endeavours, he needed to retire from the daily grind of working solely for money at a young age.

He started an export business from scratch, using the knowledge he had gained from a previous job in the industry. His intelligence and unique approach to business led to great success in a short period of time, earning him more in just a decade and a half than he would have in a lifetime working in a government job. Upon the passing of Dr. APJ Abdul Kalam, Dr. Pillai decided to leave the business and dedicate himself to reading, studying, researching, and experimenting.

During his tenure in the export business, Dr. Pillai traveled to over 16 countries, gaining valuable insight and experiencing the world and life in detail.

Dr. Pillai has achieved four Guinness World Records in the following subjects:

"Script to Screen" - In this record, Dr. Pillai produced and directed an animation film within the shortest time possible, breaking the previous record set by Canadians. He has also received numerous national and international awards and recognitions for this achievement.

Longest Line of Postcards - For this record, Dr. Pillai created a line of 16,300 postcards on the occasion of the 163rd anniversary of Indian Postal Day. The event also included a questionnaire about the Indian flag.

Largest Poster Awareness Campaign - Dr. Pillai designed an awareness campaign on the subject of "Beti Bachao - Beti Padhao" (Save the Girl Child - Educate the Girl Child) to achieve this record.

Largest Envelope - In tribute to the Indian Prime Minister's "Make in India" initiative, Dr. Pillai created a 4000 square meter envelope using waste paper to achieve this record.

Attempted - **70000 Candles on a 210 kg Cake** - To celebrate the 70th Indian Independence Day, Dr. Pillai attempted to light 70,000 candles on a 210 kg cake, which was recorded in World Records India.

Attempted - **Documentary on Dhamek Stupa of Sarnath in 17 Languages** - Dr. Pillai attempted to create a documentary on the Dhamek Stupa of Sarnath, dubbing it in 17 different languages. The result of this attempt is currently awaiting confirmation from the Guinness World Records.

Dr. Pillai is skilled in teaching the Bhagavad Gita, a Hindu scripture, and is popular among young people. He has helped many young people improve their lives through his motivational teachings.

In addition to teaching, he has composed and sung numerous Sanskrit Bhajans and patriotic songs.

He has also written and directed several short films and documentaries for awareness campaigns, and has volunteered with the police in both UP and Kerala to spread awareness about various issues through videos and photography.

Incredibly, he has produced and directed over 100 documentaries about the city of Varanasi, all on his own.

He has also helped and guided more than 25 boys and girls to achieve world records through creative and innovative methods. He is a multifaceted person who uses his intellect and the blessings given to him by God to excel in various areas. He is both a teacher and a student, always learning and teaching, and is able to master any subject he comes across.

He is a selfless social activist and motivational speaker who has overcome struggles and failures to become a successful and enthusiastic individual with a rich life experience.

In addition to his work with the Bhagavad Gita, he is also an efficient Tarot card reader, Astro-Vastu consultant, and a talented singer and composer. He has sung the entire Ram Charita Manas and Bhagavad Gita in his own compositions, and has sung the phrase "Lokah Samastha Sukhino Bhavantu" in 50 different languages. He is currently working on a detailed and scientific study of Vedas, Upanishads, Puranas, and the Bhagavad Gita. He has also composed and sung the Hanuman Chalisa and Gayatri Mantra in 108 and 1008 different compositions, respectively.

Awards - Four Times Guinness World Records, Winner of Mahatma Gandhi Vishwa Shanti Puraskar, Mahatma Gandhi Global Peace Ambassador, Kashi Ratna Award, Dr. APJ Abdul Kalam Motivational Person of the Year 2017, Mother Teresa Award, Indira Gandhi Priyadarshini Award, Bharat Vikas Ratna Award, Udyog Ratna Award, Vigyan Prasar Award, Poorvanchal Ratn Samman.

PREFACE

The Creative Mind: An Exploration of the Secrets to Unleash Your Creativity is a book that seeks to unlock the mysteries of creativity and provide readers with the tools to unleash their own creative potential. Through a combination of research, personal anecdotes, and practical advice, this book will provide readers with the knowledge and confidence to explore their own creative capabilities.

This book is for anyone who has ever felt stuck in a creative rut or has been searching for ways to tap into their own creative genius. Whether you are an artist, a writer, a musician, or simply someone who wants to explore their creative side, this book will provide you with the insight and guidance you need to unlock your creative potential.

The Creative Mind is an exploration of the secrets to unleash your creativity. It is a journey of self-discovery, a guide to unlocking the power of your imagination, and a source of inspiration for anyone looking to explore their creative side. With this book, you will gain the knowledge and confidence to unleash your creative potential and explore the depths of your creative mind.

I

Understanding Creativity and Its Importance in Unlocking Your Potential

Creativity is a powerful force that has the ability to unlock our greatest potential and bring forth innovative ideas and solutions to complex problems. It is a complex and multi-faceted concept that encompasses a range of skills and abilities, from imaginative thinking and problem-solving to the ability to express ourselves in unique and original ways. Understanding creativity and its role in our lives is essential for unlocking our full potential and achieving success in a rapidly changing world.

In this chapter, we will explore the meaning of creativity, its key components, and the benefits it offers in terms of personal and professional growth. We will also examine the ways in which creativity can be fostered and developed, as well as some of the common barriers and challenges that may arise along the way. By the end of this chapter, you will have a deeper understanding of creativity and its importance in helping you to unleash your full potential.

What is Creativity?

Creativity is a unique and individual process that allows us to generate new and innovative ideas and solutions. It involves the ability to think outside the box and see the world in new and different ways, as well as the skills and techniques necessary to bring these ideas to life. Creativity is not limited to artists and writers, but rather is a quality that can be found in people from all walks of life and in a variety of fields, from business and science to education and technology.

Components of Creativity

There are several key components of creativity, including imagination, divergent thinking, convergent thinking, and the ability to express oneself. Imagination is the ability to think beyond what is currently known and to envision new and innovative possibilities. Divergent thinking is the process of generating multiple ideas and solutions to a problem, while convergent thinking involves taking these ideas and narrowing them down to find the best possible solution. The ability to express oneself is crucial for creativity as it allows us to communicate our ideas and solutions to others.

Benefits of Creativity

Creativity offers a range of benefits, both personal and professional. On a personal level, it can help to boost self-confidence and self-esteem, foster emotional well-being, and enhance overall life satisfaction. Creativity can also lead to greater professional success, as it allows individuals to bring new and innovative ideas to the table, resulting in better decision-making, problem-solving, and team collaboration.

Fostering Creativity

Creativity can be fostered and developed through a range of activities and experiences. Engaging in creative pursuits, such as art, writing, or music, can help to stimulate the imagination and build confidence in expressing oneself. Encouraging creativity in others can also be beneficial, as this helps to create a supportive environment that fosters innovation and encourages new ideas. Additionally, taking risks and embracing uncertainty can help to build resilience and foster a more creative mindset.

Barriers to Creativity

Despite its many benefits, creativity can also face numerous barriers and challenges. One of the most common obstacles is a lack of self-confidence, which can result in individuals being too afraid to take risks and express themselves in new and innovative ways. Another barrier is a lack of time and resources, which can make it difficult to engage in creative pursuits. Finally, negative feedback from others can also stifle creativity and discourage individuals from pursuing their passions.

Creativity is a powerful force that can help individuals to unleash their full potential and achieve greater success in both their personal and professional lives. Understanding the components and benefits of creativity, as well as the ways in which it can be fostered and developed, is essential for unlocking one's full creative potential. By embracing our imagination and taking risks, we can overcome common barriers and challenges and bring forth innovative ideas and solutions to the world.

It is important to remember that creativity is not limited to a select few, but rather is a quality that can be found in individuals from all backgrounds and walks of life. By embracing our creativity, we can tap into our full potential and lead a more fulfilling and meaningful life.

In this book, we will delve deeper into the secrets of unlocking your creativity and explore the various ways in which you can develop and enhance your imaginative thinking and problem-solving skills. Through a combination of practical tips and inspiring stories, you will learn how to unleash your full creative potential and bring your unique ideas and solutions to the world. So, let's begin our journey into the creative mind and unlock your full potential today!

"Creativity is the greatest form of freedom."

൧

II

Setting Creative Goals and Creating a Plan

One of the key steps in unleashing your full creative potential is setting clear and achievable goals for your creative pursuits. A well-defined plan can help you to focus your efforts and provide direction as you work towards achieving your creative aspirations. In this chapter, we will explore the process of setting creative goals and creating a plan to help you reach your full creative potential.

Setting Creative Goals

The first step in unleashing your creative potential is to set specific and achievable goals for your creative pursuits. This might involve setting a goal to write a novel, start a new art project, or to improve your photography skills. The key to setting effective creative goals is to make them specific, measurable, achievable, relevant, and time-bound.

Once you have set your goals, it is important to break them down into smaller, more manageable steps. This will help you to focus your efforts and track your progress towards achieving your creative aspirations. For example, if your goal is to write a novel, you might break this down into smaller steps such as writing a certain number of pages each day, researching your topic, and creating a rough outline of your story.

Creating a Plan

Once you have set your creative goals, it is important to create a plan to help you reach them. A well-defined plan will help you to focus your efforts, prioritize your tasks, and overcome any obstacles that may arise along the way.

One effective way to create a plan is to use the SMART method, which involves setting Specific, Measurable, Achievable, Relevant, and Time-bound goals. By breaking down your creative goals into smaller, manageable steps, you can focus your efforts and track your progress towards achieving your creative aspirations.

Another key aspect of creating a plan is to identify any resources or support that you may need along the way. This might include taking courses or workshops, seeking feedback from others, or joining a creative community. Having the right resources and support in place can help you to stay motivated and overcome any challenges that may arise along the way.

Staying Focused and Motivated

One of the biggest challenges of achieving creative goals is staying focused and motivated over time. To overcome this challenge, it is important to establish a regular routine and set aside dedicated time each day for your creative pursuits. Additionally, it is important to celebrate your achievements and stay positive, even in the face of setbacks or challenges.

Finally, it is important to stay open to new ideas and opportunities, as this can help you to grow and develop your creative skills over time. By embracing new challenges and experimenting with new techniques, you can continue to push the boundaries of your creative abilities and unleash your full potential.

Setting creative goals and creating a plan are key steps in unleashing your full creative potential. By setting specific and achievable goals, breaking them down into smaller steps, and creating a plan, you can focus your efforts, prioritize your tasks, and achieve your creative aspirations. Additionally, staying focused, motivated, and open to new ideas can help you to grow and develop your creative skills over time, ultimately allowing you to unleash your full potential.

"Creativity is intelligence having fun."

- Albert Einstein

ॐ

III

Building a Daily Routine for Creativity

Developing a daily routine that nurtures your creativity can be a powerful tool in unlocking your full potential. A daily routine can provide structure, focus, and discipline to your creative pursuits, helping you to stay motivated and achieve your creative aspirations. In this chapter, we will explore the benefits of building a daily routine for creativity and provide tips for creating a routine that works for you.

The Benefits of a Daily Routine for Creativity

There are numerous benefits to building a daily routine for creativity, including:

Improved focus: *Having a set schedule for your creative pursuits can help you to focus your efforts and minimize* *distractions.*

Increased productivity: *By dedicating a specific amount of time each day to your creative pursuits, you can increase your overall productivity and achieve your creative goals more efficiently.*

Better time management:*A daily routine can help you to better manage your time and prioritize your creative pursuits.*

Increased motivation:*When you have a set schedule for your creative pursuits, it can be easier to stay motivated and avoid procrastination.*

Creating a Daily Routine for Creativity

When creating a daily routine for creativity, there are several key elements to consider, including:

Dedicating a specific amount of time each day to your creative pursuits: *This could be as little as 30 minutes or as much as several hours, depending on your schedule and the demands of your life.*

Making time for self-care: *Self-care activities, such as exercise, meditation, and adequate sleep, are essential for maintaining a healthy body and mind, which are key components of unlocking your full creative potential.*

Staying organized: *Keeping your creative workspace organized and clutter-free can help you to focus your efforts and minimize distractions.*

Incorporating different types of activities into your routine: *Mixing up your creative pursuits with different activities, such as writing, painting, drawing, or sculpting, can help you to stay motivated and avoid burnout.*

Tips for Success

When building a daily routine for creativity, there are several tips that can help you to be successful, including:

Making time for yourself: *It is important to prioritize your creative pursuits and make time for yourself each day.*

Staying flexible: *While having a set routine is important, it is also important to be flexible and adapt to changes as needed.*

Holding yourself accountable:*Set achievable goals and hold yourself accountable for making progress towards those goals each day.*

Celebrating your successes:*Take time to celebrate your achievements, no matter how small, to stay motivated and focused on your creative pursuits.*

Building a daily routine for creativity is a powerful tool in unlocking your full potential. By dedicating a specific amount of time each day to your creative pursuits, making time for self-care, staying organized, and incorporating different types of activities into your routine, you can stay motivated and achieve your creative goals efficiently. With these tips, you can build a routine that works for you and unleash your full creative potential.

"Creativity is a wild mind and a disciplined eye."

- Dorothy Parker

&

IV

Overcoming Creative Blocks and Staying Inspired

At some point, every creative person will face a creative block – a period of time when inspiration seems to have run dry and the ideas just don't seem to be flowing. Overcoming creative blocks can be challenging, but with the right tools and mindset, it is possible to get through it and come out stronger on the other side. In this chapter, we will explore the causes of creative blocks, and provide tips for overcoming them and staying inspired.

The Causes of Creative Blocks

There are several causes of creative blocks, including:

Burnout:

Overworking and pushing yourself too hard can lead to burnout, which can cause a temporary lack of motivation and creativity.

Fear of failure:

Fearing that your ideas will not meet your expectations or those of others can cause a block in your creative process.

Lack of inspiration:

Sometimes, you simply run out of ideas or feel uninspired.

Perfectionism:

The desire to make everything perfect can cause you to be overly critical of your work, which can lead to creative blocks.

Overcoming Creative Blocks

Overcoming creative blocks can be a challenging, but rewarding process. Here are some tips for overcoming creative blocks and getting back to your creative pursuits:

Take a break: Taking a break from your creative pursuits can help you to recharge your batteries and gain a fresh perspective on your work.

Experiment with new techniques: Trying out new techniques can help to shake up your creative process and spark new ideas.

Get outside your comfort zone: Pushing yourself to try new things and step outside your comfort zone can help you to grow and develop as a creative person.

Collaborate with others: Working with others can provide new perspectives, inspiration, and accountability to your creative pursuits.

Surround yourself with inspiration: Surrounding yourself with things that inspire you, such as music, art, or nature, can help to reignite your creative spark.

Staying Inspired

Staying inspired is an ongoing process, but there are several strategies that can help you to keep the inspiration flowing:

Stay curious: Keeping an open mind and a curious spirit can help you to stay inspired and find new sources of inspiration.

Surround yourself with positive people: Surrounding yourself with positive and supportive people can help you to maintain a positive outlook and stay motivated in your creative pursuits.

Embrace your failures: Embracing your failures and using them as opportunities for growth and learning can help you to stay inspired and motivated.

Celebrate your successes: Celebrating your successes, no matter how small, can help you to stay inspired and motivated.

Overcoming creative blocks and staying inspired can be challenging, but with the right tools and mindset, it is possible to get through it and come out stronger on the other side. By taking breaks, experimenting with new techniques, getting outside your comfort zone, collaborating with others, and surrounding yourself with inspiration, you can overcome creative blocks and stay motivated in your creative pursuits. With these tips, you can unleash your full creative potential and reach new heights in your creative journey.

"*Creativity is allowing yourself to make mistakes. Art is knowing which ones to keep.*"

- Scott Adams

ౚ

V

Building Mental and Physical Resilience

Being a creative person can be both rewarding and challenging. The ups and downs of the creative process can put a strain on both your mental and physical well-being. Building mental and physical resilience is an important aspect of unlocking your full creative potential. In this chapter, we will explore the importance of building mental and physical resilience, and provide tips for doing so.

The Importance of Building Mental Resilience

Mental resilience refers to the ability to cope with stress, adversity, and change in a positive and healthy way. Building mental resilience is important for creative individuals because it helps to:

Manage stress:

The creative process can be stressful at times, and having strong mental resilience can help you to manage this stress in a healthy way.

Overcome obstacles:

Creatives often face obstacles and challenges in their work, and having mental resilience can help you to overcome these challenges and continue to grow as a creative person.

Maintain a positive outlook:

Maintaining a positive outlook, even during tough times, is important for staying motivated and inspired in your creative pursuits.

Tips for Building Mental Resilience

Building mental resilience takes time and effort, but there are several strategies that can help:

Practice self-care:

Taking care of yourself, both physically and mentally, is essential for building mental resilience. This includes getting enough sleep, eating a healthy diet, and engaging in activities that bring you joy and relaxation.

Develop a positive mindset:

Cultivating a positive mindset, such as gratitude and

optimism, can help you to stay motivated and inspired in the face of adversity.

Set achievable goals:

Setting achievable goals and celebrating your successes, no matter how small, can help you to maintain a positive outlook and build mental resilience.

Seek support:

Surrounding yourself with positive, supportive people and seeking help when you need it can help you to build mental resilience and manage stress in a healthy way.

The Importance of Building Physical Resilience

Physical resilience refers to the ability to maintain physical health and well-being, even during periods of stress or change. Building physical resilience is important for creative individuals because it helps to:

Maintain energy levels:

Having high energy levels is essential for staying motivated and productive in your creative pursuits.

Overcome obstacles:

Maintaining physical health and wellness can help you to overcome obstacles and challenges in your creative journey.

Manage stress:

Engaging in physical activity and exercise can help to manage stress and improve mental health.

Tips for Building Physical Resilience

Building physical resilience takes time and effort, but there are several strategies that can help:

Engage in regular physical activity:

Regular physical activity, such as exercise, yoga, or meditation, can help to improve physical health and manage stress.

Eat a healthy diet:

Eating a well-balanced diet, rich in nutrients and antioxidants, can help to improve energy levels and physical well-being.

Get enough sleep:

Getting enough sleep is essential for maintaining physical health and energy levels.

Manage stress:

Engaging in activities that help to manage stress, such as deep breathing, mindfulness, or exercise, can help to improve physical resilience.

Building mental and physical resilience is an essential

aspect of unlocking your full creative potential. By practicing self-care, developing a positive mindset, engaging in regular physical activity, eating a healthy diet, getting enough sleep, and seeking support when needed, you can build the resilience you need to overcome obstacles and stay motivated in your creative pursuits. By taking the time to build mental and physical resilience, you can unleash your full creative potential and achieve your creative goals.

Remember, building resilience is not a one-time process, it requires consistent effort and a commitment to self-improvement. The benefits of building resilience are numerous and include increased energy levels, improved mental health, and a positive outlook on life. So, make building mental and physical resilience a priority in your life and watch as your creativity flourishes.

In this chapter, we have explored the importance of building mental and physical resilience and provided tips for doing so. However, it is important to remember that everyone is different, and what works for one person may not work for another. It is up to you to experiment with different strategies and find what works best for you. By doing so, you can build the resilience you need to unleash your full creative potential and achieve your creative goals.

"Creativity is a renewable resource; the more
you use, the more you have."

୫

VI

Experimenting with Different Creative Techniques

One of the keys to unlocking your creative potential is to be open to new experiences and ideas. This means being willing to try different creative techniques and see what resonates with you. There is no right or wrong way to be creative, and there are countless techniques to choose from. In this chapter, we will explore some of the most popular and effective techniques for unlocking your creativity.

Mind Mapping:

This technique involves creating a visual representation of your ideas and thoughts. Start by writing down a central idea or problem you want to solve. Then, create branches from the central idea that represent related ideas or solutions. This technique can help you organize your thoughts and identify new connections between ideas.

Freewriting:

This is a technique where you write without stopping for a set amount of time, typically 10-15 minutes. The goal is to write without worrying about grammar, spelling, or punctuation. This technique can help you tap into your subconscious mind and generate new ideas.

Brainstorming:

This is a group technique where individuals share their ideas and build off of each other's thoughts. Brainstorming is a great way to generate a large number of ideas and get feedback from others.

Artistic Expression:

Whether it be painting, drawing, sculpting, or any other form of artistic expression, creating something with your hands can be a powerful way to tap into your creativity.

Music:

Listening to music, composing your own music, or playing an instrument can all be ways to unleash your creativity. Music has the power to evoke emotions and inspire new ideas.

Meditation:

Meditation is a technique that involves focusing your mind and calming your thoughts. This can be a great way to clear your mind and tap into your inner creativity.

Nature:

Spending time in nature can provide a sense of peace and inspiration. Taking a walk in the park, sitting by a river, or going on a hike can all help you connect with your creative side.

These are just a few of the many creative techniques you can experiment with. The key is to try new things and see what resonates with you. By doing so, you can find new ways to unleash your creative potential and achieve your creative goals.

Creativity is an essential part of the human experience, and experimenting with different creative techniques is one of the keys to unlocking your full potential. Don't be afraid to try new things, and remember that there is no right or wrong way to be creative. The most important thing is to have fun and enjoy the process.

"Creativity is the power to connect the seemingly unconnected."

- William Plomer

VII

Building a Support System and Connecting with Others

One of the most important things you can do to unleash your creativity is to build a support system and connect with others. Having a support system in place can provide you with encouragement, motivation, and a sounding board for your ideas. In this chapter, we will explore the importance of building a support system and how to connect with others in the creative community.

Surround yourself with positive people:

Surrounding yourself with positive, supportive people is one of the best things you can do to unleash your creativity. These people can provide you with encouragement, motivation, and a sounding board for your ideas. Seek out friends, family members, or colleagues who are supportive of your creative pursuits.

Join a creative community:

Joining a creative community, whether online or in person, is a great way to connect with others who share your passions. This can provide you with a supportive network of like-minded individuals who can offer advice, feedback, and encouragement.

Collaborate with others:

Collaborating with others can be a great way to bring new perspectives and ideas to your work. Seek out opportunities to collaborate with others on projects, and be open to new ideas and approaches.

Attend events and workshops:

Attending events and workshops can provide you with an opportunity to connect with others in the creative community. This can be a great way to learn new techniques, get feedback on your work, and find inspiration.

Hire a coach or mentor:

Hiring a coach or mentor can be a great way to receive personalized support and guidance as you work to unleash your creativity. A coach or mentor can provide you with feedback on your work, help you set goals, and hold you accountable.

Seek feedback from others:

Seeking feedback from others is a great way to get a fresh perspective on your work. Ask friends, family members, or other creatives for their thoughts on your work, and be open to constructive criticism.

Building a support system and connecting with others is essential to unleashing your creative potential. Having a network of supportive individuals can provide you with encouragement, motivation, and a sounding board for your ideas. So, make it a priority to build a support system and connect with others in the creative community.

Creativity is a social process, and building a support system and connecting with others is essential to unlocking your full potential. Seek out positive relationships, join creative communities, collaborate with others, attend events and workshops, hire a coach or mentor, and seek feedback from others. By doing so, you can create a network of supportive individuals who can help you achieve your creative goals.

"*Creativity is the ability to see the world in a new way.*"

- *Edward de Bono*

VIII

Understanding and Managing Creative Anxiety

Creative anxiety is a common challenge for many people who are pursuing their creative passions. This anxiety can stem from a variety of sources, including fear of failure, fear of judgment, or a lack of confidence in one's abilities. In this chapter, we will explore creative anxiety and provide strategies for managing and overcoming it.

Recognize the signs of creative anxiety:

Understanding the signs of creative anxiety is the first step in managing it. Some common symptoms of creative anxiety include procrastination, self-doubt, and avoidance behaviors. If you are experiencing these symptoms, it is important to take them seriously and seek help.

Embrace the fear:

Embracing the fear that comes with creative anxiety can be a powerful tool for managing it. Instead of avoiding your fears, try to confront them head-on. This can help you develop a sense of resilience and increase your confidence in your abilities.

Practice mindfulness:

Mindfulness can be a powerful tool for managing creative anxiety. Mindfulness involves focusing on the present moment and accepting your thoughts and feelings without judgment. This can help you stay calm and focused, even in the face of anxiety.

Seek professional help:

If your creative anxiety is severe or interfering with your ability to pursue your creative passions, it may be necessary to seek professional help. A therapist can help you identify the root causes of your anxiety and provide you with strategies for managing it.

Get support from others:

Getting support from others can be a great way to manage creative anxiety. Seek out a support group, join a creative community, or connect with a mentor or coach who can provide you with encouragement and support.

Set realistic goals:

Setting realistic goals for your creative work can help reduce anxiety by giving you a sense of direction and purpose. Be mindful of what you can realistically achieve in a given time frame, and don't be afraid to adjust your goals as needed.

Celebrate your successes:

Celebrating your successes, no matter how small, can help you develop a sense of pride and confidence in your abilities. This can help reduce creative anxiety and increase your overall well-being.

Creative anxiety is a common challenge for many people who are pursuing their creative passions. However, by recognizing the signs of creative anxiety, embracing the fear, practicing mindfulness, seeking professional help, getting support from others, setting realistic goals, and celebrating your successes, you can effectively manage and overcome creative anxiety. With the right tools and support, you can unleash your full creative potential and achieve your goals.

"*Creativity is the ability to find new solutions to old problems*"

IX

The Power of Positive Thinking and Gratitude

Positive thinking and gratitude are two of the most powerful tools we have to unlock our creativity. By focusing on the positive aspects of our lives, we can open ourselves up to new possibilities and ideas. Gratitude, on the other hand, helps us to appreciate the good things in our lives and to recognize the abundance that surrounds us.

When we combine positive thinking and gratitude, we can create a powerful force that can help us to unlock our creative potential. Positive thinking helps us to focus on the good things in our lives and to recognize the opportunities that are available to us. Gratitude helps us to appreciate the abundance that we have and to recognize the beauty in the world around us.

When we combine these two powerful forces, we can create a powerful mindset that can help us to unlock our creative potential. We can use positive thinking to focus on the good things in our lives and to recognize the opportunities that are available to us. We can use gratitude to appreciate the abundance that we have and to recognize the beauty in the world around us.

By combining positive thinking and gratitude, we can create a powerful mindset that can help us to unlock our creative potential. We can use this mindset to focus on the good things in our lives and to recognize the opportunities that are available to us. We can use it to appreciate the abundance that we have and to recognize the beauty in the world around us. With this mindset, we can open ourselves up to new possibilities and ideas, and we can create a powerful force that can help us to unleash our creativity.

The power of positive thinking and gratitude are often overlooked and underestimated, yet both play a large role in a person's emotional and physical well-being. Positive thinking and gratitude can increase resilience, inspire creativity, and improve overall mental and physical health.

Positive thinking is the belief that one's thoughts and behaviors can either positively or negatively affect their interaction with the world. It is the belief that one has the power to turn any negative situation into a positive one, and that it is possible to learn from every experience and use it towards betterment. According to research, positive thinking can reduce the risk of mental illnesses and encourage recovery from physical illnesses. Additionally, it can help increase self-esteem, reduce stress, and improve one's outlook on life.

Gratitude is the feeling of appreciation for what one has and what one receives. It is the recognition that life is full of experiences, both good and bad, and those experiences should be appreciated. Gratitude can make difficult times easier to bear and can be a great source of strength and resilience in the face of adversity. It also allows one to focus on the positive things in life, instead of dwelling on the negative. It encourages joy, contentment, and humbleness. Additionally, research shows that thankfulness can improve physical health, including sleep quality, immune function, and heart health.

Although positive thinking and gratitude are immensely beneficial, it can be difficult to maintain them both in times of difficulty. It is important to remember that life has ups and downs, and the best way to deal with those difficulties is by accepting them and learning from them. Additionally, engaging in activities that one finds enjoyable and that promote positivity, such as reading, writing, or other forms of self-expression, can be helpful in instilling gratitude and positive thinking.

In conclusion, positive thinking and gratitude are essential for a fulfilling life. They play a large role in resilience, creativity, and mental and physical health. By recognizing the power of both and actively engaging in activities to foster positivity, one can experience a higher sense of joy and contentment.

"Creativity is the process of bringing something new into being."

- Twyla Tharp

X

Dealing with Failure and Learning from Mistakes

When it comes to creative thinkers and innovators, dealing with failure and learning from mistakes are key elements of success. Learning from mistakes is essential for creative thinkers to grow and develop as individuals, and to explore new creative opportunities. In order to effectively deal with failure and learn from mistakes, creative thinkers must be open to constructive feedback, identify the areas of improvement, and actively seek out new opportunities for growth.

Constructive feedback provides valuable insight for successful creative thinkers. When a creative thinker encounters failure, it is important to solicit feedback from others in order to gain a better understanding of what went wrong and identify potential areas of improvement. Creative thinkers must also be mindful to actively listen to the feedback they receive and embrace it as an opportunity to grow and move on from any mistakes made. Additionally, feedback should be used to formulate action plans and strategies to make the necessary changes needed to progress while avoiding any future failure.

The second step to learning from past mistakes is to identify areas of improvement. After receiving feedback, creative thinkers should be able to reflect and self-evaluate. It is essential to critically assess all aspects of a past failure in order to understand what went wrong, identify any problems that caused it, and formulate solutions for avoiding similar issues in the future. By taking the time to analyze and observe patterns, creative thinkers can gain a better understanding of the creative process and prevent any future roadblocks.

Failure is an inevitable part of life, and it can be a difficult experience to process. It can be tempting to give up and feel discouraged, but it is important to remember that failure is an opportunity to learn and grow. It is a chance to reflect on what went wrong and to make changes that will help you succeed in the future.

The first step in learning from failure is to accept it. It is important to recognize that failure is a part of life and that it is not a reflection of your worth as a person. Once you have accepted failure, you can begin to look at it objectively and identify what went wrong. This can help you to understand why you failed and to identify areas for improvement.

The next step is to take action. Once you have identified the areas that need improvement, you can begin to make changes. This could involve changing your approach, learning new skills, or seeking help from others. Taking action will help you to move forward and to make progress towards your goals.

Then, it is important to remember that failure is not the end of the journey. It is a part of the creative process and can be used as a learning experience. By reflecting on your mistakes and taking action, you can use failure to your advantage and become a better creative.

Failure can be a difficult experience, but it is an essential part of the creative journey. By accepting failure, looking at it objectively, and taking action, you can use it to your advantage and become a better creative. With the right attitude and approach, failure can be a powerful tool to help you reach your goals.

Finally, creative thinkers should actively seek out new opportunities for learning and growth. When it comes to creative thinking and innovation, there is always something new to learn and explore. Creative thinkers should take the initiative to research new methods and techniques to remain current with industry trends and make sure that their skills are relevant to the current market. Additionally, creative thinkers should make sure to challenge themselves and push past their comfort zones in order to experience growth and continually improve their skills.

In conclusion, dealing with failure and learning from mistakes are essential skills for creative thinkers and innovators. Learning from mistakes is the key to success, and creative thinkers must be open to feedback, identify any potential areas of improvement, and proactively seek out new opportunities for learning and growth. By adopting this approach, creative thinkers will be able to effectively identify and overcome any potential flaws, and consistently improve over time.

"Creativity is the courage to let go of certainties."

- Erich Fromm

XI

Finding and Pursuing Your Creative Passions

There is no single right way to unleash your creative passions, but there are plenty of ways to approach the challenge. Finding and pursuing your creative passions can be a rewarding journey, one that can provide immense personal satisfaction and fulfillment. To achieve such a goal, it is important to take the time to explore and identify what interests you; learning what motivates and excites you is essential to finding and pursuing your passions.

Once you have identified potential creative passions, it is important to set realistic goals for yourself. Take the time to reflect and create a timeline for yourself; setting deadlines for each step you take allows you to keep track of your progress and motivates you to continue working towards your goals. Doing so will also help you create a road map that can be adjusted as you move forward and explore new interests.

To further unlock your creative passions, it is also important to take risks. Challenging yourself can help you discover entirely new creative possibilities; don't be afraid to ask questions and reach outside of your comfort zone. Additionally, having a support system of like-minded individuals can offer a helping hand when the creative process becomes overwhelming. Whether keeping in touch with a friend over the phone or joining an online creative community, it pays to surround yourself with people who can inspire and offer advice.

At the same time, it is essential that you take care of yourself during this process as well. Staying rested and fueled is an important factor in maintaining your mental and physical health. Taking breaks on a regular basis, turning off technology and tuning into your environment, and relying on family and friends for support are key components of self-care. Additionally, staying active and partaking in activities and hobbies that bring you pleasure can improve the quality of your work.

It is important to note that the process of finding and pursuing your creative passions is unique to each individual. Therefore, it is important to strive for progress and not perfection. Despite setbacks and bumps along the way, it is essential to continue on the path towards uncovering and indulging in your creative passions. Along the way, you are sure to experience immense personal gratification and satisfaction, as you watch each creative project come to life in front of your eyes.

The first step in finding and pursuing your creative passions is to identify what you are passionate about. Take some time to reflect on what you enjoy doing and what you are naturally drawn to. Consider activities that bring you joy and make you feel energized. Once you have identified your passions, you can begin to explore ways to pursue them.

One way to pursue your creative passions is to take classes or workshops. This can be a great way to learn new skills and gain knowledge in a particular area. Additionally, you can join a community of like-minded individuals who share your interests. This can provide you with a supportive environment to explore and develop your creative passions.

Another way to pursue your creative passions is to create a portfolio of your work. This can be a great way to showcase your skills and talents to potential employers or clients. Additionally, it can be a great way to track your progress and stay motivated.

Finally, it is important to remember that pursuing your creative passions is a journey. It is important to be patient and to take the time to enjoy the process. Additionally, it is important to be open to feedback and to take risks. With the right attitude and resources, you can find and pursue your creative passions with confidence.

"Creativity is the capacity to bring the seemingly impossible to life."

જી

XII

Understanding and Managing Perfectionism

Perfectionism can be defined as an excessive need for order, control, and accuracy, or an unrealistic belief that one must achieve perfection in order to be successful. It can manifest itself in different ways, such as procrastination, fear of failure, and an inability to accept criticism.

Perfectionism is a complex psychological trait that can manifest in a variety of ways and exert significant influence over an individual's behavior, emotions, and self-concept. Not only does it have potential to fuel creativity, but it can also stifle it if not managed properly. Learning to harness perfectionism in order to maximize success and unlock its power as a tool of creativity is imperative.

One key issue with managing perfectionism is to recognize

and address the difference between productive and self-defeating perfectionism. Productive perfectionism is healthily aimed at seeking personal excellence and striving for positive outcomes and results. Self-defeating perfectionism, on the other hand, tends to be driven by fear, anxiety, and potentially unrealistic standards. As such, it can lead to feelings of failure and discouragement.

One of the most important ingredients to unlocking the creative potential of perfectionism and effectively managing it is cultivating self-compassion and being more mindful of the present moment. Taking steps to be aware of and accept one's own flaws and shortcomings can help quell the fear of failure associated with perfectionism and create the space for unleashing creativity.

Additionally, it is beneficial to practice rigorous yet realistic goal-setting. Having a clear direction and an attainable roadmap will help to better manage expectations, give clarity on progress and foster a sense of accomplishment as opposed to feeling of action and subsequent inaction. A step-by-step approach is often suggested for managing perfectionism and achieving goals successfully.

Finally, it is critical to allow for mistakes and be proactive in embracing failure. Recognizing that failure is a part of the creative process, taking risks, and allowing for opportunities to experiment and learn, can be stimulating and refreshing. Making room for failure will ultimately pave the way for positive risk-taking and encourage creative growth.

Understanding and managing perfectionism can be key to

releasing creativity and achieving success. Engaging in mindful self-reflection and self-compassion, setting realistic goals, and welcoming failure as part of the creative process are all essential components of unlocking one's creative potential. With these steps, perfectionism can become an effective tool of creativity rather than an obstacle to be overcome.

"*Creativity is the ability to combine existing ideas in new ways.*"

৪৩

XIII

Building Self-Compassion and Embracing Vulnerability

Creativity is a valuable tool for success in many areas of life, from studying, to art, to business. Self-compassion is a key component necessary to having a creative mind. It is vital to have self-compassion in order to view creativity as something that is achievable and can be improved upon. Without self-compassion, it becomes difficult to be creative, because creativity is not perfect, and perfectionism can become a barrier to creating something new.

Self-compassion is essential in aiding individuals in navigating the natural ups and downs of life. Self-compassion is an attitude of kindness and consideration towards oneself. It is distinguished by three core components: self-kindness, common humanity, and mindfulness. Self-kindness is the focus on gentleness and understanding towards oneself and any mistakes or failures. Common humanity is the knowledge and understanding that all humans go through hardships and that suffering is normal and shared. Finally, mindfulness is the non-judgemental awareness of difficult emotions and situations.

Self-compassion can help an individual become more creative in their thinking. It can help create an open andgrowth-minded environment, instead of an environment of perfectionism and comparison. Self-compassion allows individuals to viewfailures and mistakes more objectively, instead of taking mistakes personally. Mistakes no longer become seen as reflections of their personal worth, but rather as information for improvement. It allows individuals to more easily let go of any emotional blocks that come up, which aids creative flow.

Self-compassion also helps decrease social comparison by allowing one to better accept their individuality. It promotes an internal sense of security and safety, while providing individuals with the emotional resources necessary to open up to their own unique perspective and creativity.

In order to increase self-compassion, it can be beneficial to practice mindfulness and to turn any negative self-talk into self-kindness. It helps to be aware of one's own thoughts and feelings in order to be better equipped to respond with self-compassionate attitudes. Additionally, self-compassion involves taking breaks and having self-care, such as going for a walk, listening to music, or having a nap.

In conclusion, self-compassion is a valuable skill necessary for developing a creative mind. It involves viewing failures objectively, understanding that mistakes are expected, and responding to all emotions with self-kindness. To increase self-compassion, it can be beneficial to practice mindfulness, be aware of thoughts, and to have self-care. When practiced diligently, self-compassion can foster creative thinking, allowing individuals to become more creative in all aspects of their life.

"Creativity is the spark that ignites innovation."

છ

XIV

The Role of Mindfulness in Creativity

The mind is a powerful tool, capable of solving puzzles, providing creative solutions to problems and innovating new ideas and products. In order to effectively utilize the minds creative capabilities, it is important to practice mindfulness. Mindfulness is the conscious practice of being aware of the present moment, and understanding one's thoughts, feelings and environment. This practice can become an essential ingredient in developing a creative mindset.

The first step in becoming more mindful is to develop the practice of being aware of one's own thoughts, feelings and sensations. Learning to observe these internal experiences becomes a foundation for being present and present in the moment. This includes monitoring one's environment, thoughts and emotions. As you begin to monitor these experiences, you become more aware of the external environment and your underlying thoughts. Noticing these aspects can at times bring up uncomfortable feelings or strong emotions, however this practice of bringing awareness to our inner experience allows us to better relate to and understand our environment. This in turn can set the conditions to be more productive, creative and able to think critically.

The next step in developing mindfulness is to apply it to creative problem solving. Mindfulness can provide an avenue for insight into our thought patterns and patterns of behavior which can unlock creative solutions and ideas. Here, mindfulness can be used to be aware of the thought processes behind our ideas. It is also an effective tool for breaking down challenging problems and understanding the root causes. In this way, mindfulness helps to create a more in-depth understanding of our environment, leading to more innovative ideas and possibilities.

The final step in developing a creative mind is to apply mindfulness to the process of implementing creative ideas. Often those with creative ideas struggle to successfully complete their projects or get discouraged when ideas don't manifest the way they expected. Mindfulness helps creative thinkers to stay grounded in their process and focus on the specific tasks at hand without getting overwhelmed by the big picture. Being mindful can help to break down seemingly difficult projects in achievable steps and make the task of implementation more manageable.

Mindfulness is an essential practice in developing a creative mindset. By being present in the moment and aware of one's internal thought processes and environment, mindfulness allows for an increased depth of understanding leading to more creative problem solving. Furthermore, mindfulness can be used to organize tasks and stay with the creative process for successful implementation. Mindfulness helps to unlock the mind's potential for creativity and innovation, making it an invaluable tool in developing a creative mindset.

"*Creativity is the fuel that drives progress.*"

଼

XV
Unlocking Your Creative Potential

Creativity can be a powerful tool to unlock one's potential and to develop a creative mind. Many believe creativity is something we are born with, but through dedication and practice it can also be nurtured and grown. To discover one's inner creativity, uncovering it through a combination of self-exploration and practical measures can be a great help.

One of the first steps in unlocking one's creative potential is to open one's mind and accept failure. Sometimes, coming up with a new, unique idea can be overwhelming, and this fear can limit the creative possibilities. Dismissing the fear of failure and allowing oneself the space to learn and explore can open up worlds of possibilities that previously felt unattainable. An open mind also allows for new perspectives and solutions, making new solutions to existing problems much easier.

Maintaining a creative journal is one way to ensure one's creative ideas are carefully documented and can be referred back to later. Writing down ideas and thoughts can help capture the creative impulse when it strikes and provide an outlet for self-expression. This can be especially helpful for individuals who are simply beginning to explore their creative potential and don't yet have the skills to express their ideas through practical means.

Practicing creative activities such as painting, drawing, sculpting and even writing can also be beneficial in unlocking one's potential. Taking the time to explore and practice different mediums helps to sharpen one's creative skills and express oneself in different ways. Additionally, studying and learning about the works of other creatives—whether it is reading a book or attending an gallery—helps to expand one's creative horizons and inspire further creativity.

In order to tap into and unlock a creative mind, one must practice, experiment and remain open to creative possibility. Focusing on the creative process and removing any competitive element can help to make the creative journey more enjoyable and effective. Ultimately, taking the initiative to foster creativity can help unlock an individual's fullest potential, developing a creative mind and creating a bright, vibrant future.

"*Creativity is the key to unlocking your potential.*"

ॐ

OTHER BOOKS OF THE AUTHOR

1. The Moments When I Met God
2. Kashiyile Theertha Pathangal
3. Guru Gyan Vani
4. Abhiprerak Gita
5. Assi Se Jain Ghat Tak
6. Hopelessness Of Arjuna
7. The Soul And It's True Nature
8. Sense Of Action (Karma)
9. Action Through Wisdom
10. Action Through Wisdom
11. Theory And Practical Of Every Action
12. Logical Understanding Of The Supreme
13. The Imperishable Supreme
14. Yatra Nishadraj Se Hanuman Ghat Tak
15. Yatra Karnatak Ghat Se Raja Ghat Tak
16. Yatra Pandey Ghat Se Prayagraj Ghat Tak
17. Yatra Ranjendra Prasad Ghat Se Dattatreya Ghat Tak
18. Yaatrasindhiya Ghat Se Gwaliar Ghat Tak
19. Yatra Mangala Gauri Ghat Se Hanuman Gadhi Ghat Tak
20. Yatra Gaay Ghat Se Nishad Ghat Tak
21. Maa Ganga, Ghaten Evm Utsav
22. Ganga Arti Dev Deepavali Evam Any Utsav
23. Potentials Of Digitalized India
24. Vedic Consciousness
25. A Brief Introduction To Vedic Science
26. Kashi Ke Barah Jyotirling
27. Impact Of Motivation
28. Let's Have A Milky Way Journey
29. Color Therapy In A Nutshell

59. The Holistic Cow: A Look At The Physical, Spiritual, And Cultural Importance Of Cows In India
60. Arts Of Healing
61. Exploring The Divine
62. Understanding Five Elements
63. The Etymology Of Ram
64. Symbols Of India
65. Voice Of Change (About Speeches Of Great Men)
66. She Speaks (About Speeches Of Great Women)
67. Patriotism On Celluloid – Brief About Patriotic Films
68. The Music Of Motivation: A Brief Guide To Inspirational Film Songs
69. Unlocking The Secrets of The Dashopanishads
70. A Cultural Mosaic
71. Ancient Traditions, Modern Minds
72. Ecos Of Ancient Wisdom
73. Beneath The Surface
74. From Temples To Ashrams
75. Sages Of The Subcontinent
76. The Art Of Healling (Ayurveda, Yoga & Naturopathy)
77. Indian Kitchen
78. The Festivals Of India
79. The Indian Epics Retold
80. The Power Of Mantras
81. The Indian River Ganges
82. The Indian Architecture
83. Rites Of Passage
84. The Indian Silk Road
85. The Indian Literature
86. The Indian Villages
87. The Indian Folks & Crafts
88. The Way Of Buddha
89. The Ramayan Of Tulsidas

90. Astrological Remedies
91. The Secret Power Of Motivation
92. Secret Of Developing Your Inner Strength
93. The Secret Path To Motivation
94. The Art And Secret Of Positive Thinking
95. The Secrets Of Practicing Ethical Living
96. Indian Art And Painting
97. The Indian Herbalism
98. Bharatanatyam To Kathak
99. Exploring India's Astrological Remedies
100. The Indian Festival Of Flowers
101. Indian Handicrafts
102. The Splashes Of Joy – India's Colour Festival
103. The Indian Science Of Astrology
104. The Indian Mythology
105. Path To Enlightenment
106. The Indian Spirituality For Children
107. Aromas Of India
108. The Secrets Of Healthy Relationships
109. Ancestral Ties
110. The Indian Street Food
111. Discovering America
112. The Indian Textile
113. Listening To Motivational Speeches
114. Taste Of India
115. A Cultural Journey Through Indian Nuptials
116. Motivational Quote For Change
117. Secret Strategies For Making Money
118. Secrets To Cultivate A Positive Mindset
119. A Tapestry Of Cultures: Exploring India From Kashmir To Kanyakumari
120. Achieving Your Dreams With Resilience: Secret Strategies For Overcoming Obstacles

121. Innovative Startups - 25 Startup Ideas To Spark Your Business Creativity
122. Export Management: Strategies For Global Success
123. Exporting From India - A Step By Step Guide
124. Finance Fundamentals: Mastering Financial Management For Business Success
125. Global Growth Strategies For International Business Development
126. Marketing Mastery: Unlocking The Secrets Of Modern Marketing
127. Operations Mastery: Managing The Flow Of Value In Business
128. Strategic Business Management: Navigating The Modern Business Landscape
129. Human Resource Management Strategies For Building And Managing A High Performance Team
130. The Indian Landscapes And Nature: An Exploration Of India's Natural Beauty And Diversity
131. The Indian Street Performances: A Cultural Exploration Of India's Street Performances
132. Affirming Your Self-Worth: Strategies For Achieving Emotional Wellbeing
133. Cultivating Self-Discipline: Secrets Methods For Achieving Your Goals
134. Embracing Change: Strategies For Adapting To Life's Challenges
135. Embracing Your Uniqueness: Secret Strategies For Living An Authentic Life
136. Finding Motivation In Despondency: Coping With Difficult Times
137. Embracing Change
138. Learning To Love Yourself
139. Managing Time For Yourself

Contact

DR. JAGADEESH PILLAI

MBA & PhD in Vedic Science

Four Times Guinness World Record Holder

Winner of Mahatma Gandhi Vishwa Shanti Puraskar and
Global Peace Ambassador

Gemology, Astro & Vastu Consultant - Spiritual Counselor

Consultant for designing World Record Ideas

Efficient Tarot Card Reader

9839093003

myrichindia@gmail.com

drjagadeeshpillai@facebook

drjagadeeshpillai@instagram

jagadeeshpillai@youtube

www. JAGADEESHPILLAI.com

ॐ

|| LOKAHA SAMASTHAHA SUKHINO BHAVANTU ||